Effective Podcasting

Essential Elements for Success

ALESSANDRO MAZZÙ

Effective Podcasting

CONTENTS

Effective Podcasting

INTRODUCTION: WHY PODCASTING IS AN ART

Podcasting is an art that goes far beyond simply pressing 'rec' and starting to speak. It's a profound, intimate, and immersive form of communication that allows you to enter people's lives in ways that other platforms cannot offer. Think about it: your listeners tune in during very personal and private moments of their day. You are not just background noise, but a constant presence that accompanies them through their routines—while driving to work, jogging in the park, preparing dinner, or perhaps while relaxing before bed.

These intimate moments are special because your audience lets you into their lives in a way that they might not do with a video or a social media post. They don't have to stop to watch you, nor do they have to interrupt their activities: they can live their daily lives while you are with them, discreet yet constant. This is the true power of podcasting: creating an authentic, deep, and continuous connection without being intrusive or overwhelming.

The voices inhabiting this space—the podcasting world—often become more than just narrators. They become travel companions, trusted figures, familiar voices transmitting emotions, ideas, advice, or simply offering company. It's in these moments that the magic happens, as a podcast is not just a container for information but a medium through which energy, empathy, and humanity are conveyed.

Imagine your podcast as a conversation, not a lecture. Your audience is not there to learn from you passively, but to share an experience with you. They want to hear your voice, not just for what you say, but for how you say it. The tone, the rhythm, the pauses: everything contributes to creating an emotional bond that can be powerful and lasting. Every word has the power to create a world, and each episode is a new opportunity to build a relationship—a new chapter in this shared story.

But what makes a podcast truly successful? Of course, there's no magic formula. Every podcast is different, just as every podcaster is unique. However, there are certain elements that appear in the best podcasts—traits that every content creator dreaming of leaving a mark must know and master. We're not just talking about technical aspects or tools. We're referring to the deeper elements, the ones that make the difference between a podcast that gets forgotten and one that stays in people's hearts and minds.

Podcasting is a journey, and like every journey, it requires preparation, dedication, and a clear vision of where you want to go. It's not just about having the right microphone or being a good speaker. It's about understanding the nature of the art you're creating, about being aware that you are building something unique that can change the day, or even the life, of those who listen to you

1. CREATE VALUABLE CONTENT

The first and most important ingredient for a successful podcast is content. It might seem obvious, but this is where many podcasters fail. Too often, people think it's enough to talk, to fill time with words and phrases to create an episode, but in reality, this approach is a common mistake. A podcast isn't just a sequence of sounds; it's an opportunity to provide something valuable to those listening—whether it's deep reflection, a laugh, or information that can genuinely make a difference in their lives.

Think about a conversation between friends: empty, meaningless discussions are the ones you tend to forget. The ones that leave an impression, that you remember fondly, are the ones where your interlocutor said something that enriched you, made you think, or inspired you in some way. The same principle applies to podcasting. Every word you say should have weight, real value, because the people who choose to listen to you are dedicating part of their time—often precious time—to you. Their time deserves respect, and this respect is demonstrated in the way you prepare and deliver your content.

The Value of Content: Giving Shape and Substance to Your Message

Every episode of your podcast should begin with a fundamental question: "What is the goal of this episode?" Do you want to inform your audience about a topic you're an expert in? Do you want to inspire them with personal or success stories? Or maybe you just want to entertain them and provide a moment of lightness? Clearly defining the goal of each episode will help you stay focused and create coherent, valuable content.

But don't stop there. Also ask yourself: "Why should my audience listen to me?" Today, there are thousands of podcasts available on any imaginable topic. Why should they choose yours? The answer lies in the unique value you can offer. Maybe it's your storytelling style, your personal perspective on a subject, or your ability to make complex concepts understandable. Your podcast must offer something that others don't, or, if it addresses topics that others have already tackled, it must do so in a way that feels new, fresh, or more personal.

Preparing Content with Care

Once you've identified the value you want to offer, the next step is preparing your content with care. This means not relying on improvisation but instead organizing your ideas, developing a structure, and creating a clear narrative flow. This doesn't mean you have to write a script word for word, but you do need to have a well-thought-out outline that will guide you through the episode. Think about the introduction, the key points you want to touch on, and how to conclude the episode, leaving your listeners with a clear takeaway.

Content preparation also includes research. Even if you are an expert in your niche, supporting your ideas with facts, statistics, or personal experiences adds depth and credibility to your podcast. Research helps ensure that your content is accurate and relevant, and it gives you the confidence to speak authoritatively on your subject.

Storytelling as a Tool

One of the most powerful ways to deliver valuable content is through storytelling. People love stories—they're engaging, memorable, and can make complex information easier to understand. Integrating stories into your episodes, whether they're personal anecdotes or illustrative case studies, can transform dry information into something that resonates emotionally with your audience.

When telling a story, aim to create a narrative arc: a beginning, a middle, and an end. Introduce the context, present the problem or challenge, and then guide the listener through the resolution or key lesson learned. By doing this, you not only provide valuable information but also create an emotional connection with your audience, which helps strengthen their engagement with your podcast.

Consistency in Content Quality

Creating valuable content doesn't mean hitting the mark once or twice. Consistency is key to building and retaining a loyal audience. Every episode you publish should meet the same high standards of quality, both in terms of content and production. If listeners feel they can rely on you to deliver thoughtful, engaging, and valuable episodes every time, they will be more likely to stay with you over the long term.

This consistency also applies to your podcast's format and style. While experimenting with different episode lengths and formats is encouraged (as we'll discuss in later chapters), maintaining a coherent tone and approach helps reinforce your brand and keeps your listeners connected to the overall experience you offer.

In conclusion, the content of your podcast is the heart of your show. It's the reason people tune in, the reason they keep coming back. By providing valuable content, you not only fulfill the expectations of your audience but also establish yourself as a trusted voice in your niche. Content that is well-prepared, thoughtfully structured, and delivered with authenticity will always have the power to captivate, inspire, and make a lasting impact..

2. DON'T NEGLECT AUDIO

Audio is the heart of a podcast, and if you're in the podcasting world or thinking of entering it, this is a concept you can never forget. You might have heard this advice countless times, but it bears repeating: if your audio is poor, even the best content won't be listened to. You may have the brightest ideas, the most fascinating stories, or the most valuable information, but if your audience struggles to hear clearly what you're saying, you'll quickly lose their attention.

We live in an era where people's attention is incredibly fragmented. The competition to capture and retain listeners' attention is fierce. A podcast episode must compete with thousands of other content types—from YouTube videos to social media posts, television shows, and books. Even a minor technical issue can cause a listener to switch channels, and one of the primary obstacles is audio quality.

The Impact of Audio Quality on the Listening Experience

Everyone can occasionally have an episode with some background noise or record under less than ideal conditions. And yes, the audience can be forgiving, especially if it's an isolated incident. But if poor audio quality becomes a constant issue, if your podcast is characterized by distorted sounds, too-low audio levels, or annoying noises, listeners' patience will soon run out. Today's audiences have high expectations regarding sound quality. Accustomed to professional, well-produced content, listeners are less inclined to tolerate prolonged audio defects.

It's essential to understand that audio isn't just a vehicle for conveying information; it's also an integral part of the emotional experience for the listener. Clean, clear, and balanced audio creates a pleasant, relaxing, and engaging listening experience. On the other hand, disturbed audio can cause frustration, fatigue, and ultimately drive listeners away.

How Audio Affects Your Connection with the Audience

Imagine listening to a podcast while you're out for a walk or driving. You're immersed in the story the host is telling, everything flows smoothly until the audio becomes distorted or the volume suddenly drops. At that moment, all the attention you had is interrupted, and instead of focusing on the content, you start fixating on the irritation caused by the poor audio. Maybe you pause the episode, telling yourself you'll come back to it later. And you know what often happens? That 'later' never comes.

This is exactly the kind of situation that a podcaster should avoid. A listener who pauses might never return. In an age where content choices are infinite, competition is high, and even a small obstacle can cause someone to stop following a show and look for another. For this reason, audio quality should never be neglected. No matter how good your content is, if it's not pleasant to listen to, it won't be heard.

Investing in Quality Equipment: A Crucial Step

It's often thought that to achieve decent audio quality, you need a professional studio and expensive equipment. But that's not true. You don't need to spend a fortune to get good audio, but you do need to make some smart investments that will bring significant improvements. One of the key aspects is the environment in which you record. Even without a professional studio, you can drastically improve sound quality by acoustically treating your room. There are budget-friendly methods, like using portable sound-absorbing panels, heavy curtains, or rugs to reduce echo. Acoustic treatment helps eliminate sound reflections and unwanted noises, making your voice clearer and more natural.

The Importance of a Good Microphone and Audio Interface

One of the most important investments is undoubtedly the microphone. A quality microphone makes a huge difference, not only in how your voice is captured but also in the amount of editing needed afterward. Low-end microphones can make your voice sound distant, flat, or metallic, requiring much more post-production work to improve the sound. A decent microphone, however, can capture your voice more naturally and with less background noise, saving you hours of editing.

Also, make sure to use a good audio interface. Again, you don't need to buy a top-of-the-line device, but having a reliable audio interface will allow you to capture a clean recording without background noise.

The Role of Monitoring and Editing

Before you start recording, always do a few test runs. Real-time monitoring during recording allows you to detect any audio problems before they become irreversible. This means wearing studio headphones while recording to hear exactly how your voice sounds and to check for any interference or background noise. Listening in real-time will help you make necessary adjustments on the spot and avoid discovering issues only during the editing phase.

A well-done recording not only improves the listener's experience but also significantly reduces your editing time. If you record in optimal conditions, you won't have to spend hours cleaning up the audio file, eliminating unwanted noise, or trying to balance sound levels. Editing will still be an important step, of course, but it won't be a tedious and frustrating process. This will save you valuable time that you can invest in creating new content or improving other aspects of your podcast.

Audio Quality as a Sign of Respect for the Audience

Finally, think of audio quality as a sign of respect for your audience. Those who listen to you dedicate their precious time to you—time they could spend doing a thousand other things. Offering them quality audio shows that you appreciate their time and are committed to making their listening experience as enjoyable as possible. Clean, clear, and well-curated audio creates a relationship of trust with your audience. It shows that you take your work seriously and care about their experience.

In conclusion, audio is truly the beating heart of a podcast. If there's one thing you can't afford to skimp on, it's sound quality. It's not just about investing in better equipment but also understanding the importance of recording in a suitable environment, monitoring in real-time, and doing accurate editing. With high-quality audio, your podcast won't just be listened to—it will be appreciated, remembered, and most importantly, followed loyally over time.

3. BE AUTHENTIC

A podcast is not just a sequence of well-ordered words, nor is it merely the transmission of information. It's how the words are spoken, the intonation you use, the passion you convey through your voice, and most importantly, your genuine presence that can shine through even the simplest of speeches. In a world dominated by pre-packaged, overly perfected content, what truly stands out—what really grabs and holds the audience's attention—is authenticity.

When people first start podcasting, many are afraid they won't be interesting enough or that they'll make mistakes. It's easy to fall into the trap of perfectionism: thinking that to come across as professional and competent, you need to follow a script to the letter, avoid any stumbles or hesitations. But the secret of podcasting is that people don't want to listen to perfect individuals; they want to listen to real people. They want to hear your humanity, your warmth, your emotions. And here's the magic: your imperfection is what makes you interesting and memorable.

Being authentic doesn't mean improvising or speaking without any preparation, but it does mean speaking from the heart. You can prepare a script, have a guideline, but the way you deliver that message is what truly matters. The audience isn't looking for a flawless or impeccable speech; they're looking for someone to connect with, someone who can make them feel less alone, who can accompany them and make their time more enriching and meaningful. People want to listen to voices that reflect sincerity and passion, not robots coldly reading phrases.

The Fear of Being Yourself

One of the biggest fears for those approaching the world of podcasting is the fear of not being "enough." We fear that our voice isn't interesting enough, that our stories aren't engaging enough, that our thoughts don't meet expectations. This insecurity often leads us to wear a mask, trying to emulate those who have succeeded before us or to strictly follow a script. But the truth is that people connect more easily with imperfection than with perfection.

What happens when you make a mistake while speaking? Your first reaction might be to cut that part out, redo the whole segment. But stop for a moment and think: perhaps that moment of vulnerability could be exactly what makes that episode memorable. Laughing at yourself, admitting a mistake, or taking a pause to reflect doesn't make you less professional. On the contrary, it shows your audience that you're human, that you too are subject to the same mistakes and hesitations that everyone faces daily. This makes you more accessible, more relatable.

The Importance of Emotions

Emotions are the heart of a podcast. If you speak with passion, your audience will feel it. If you share a story that deeply touched you, those listening will be moved as well. But if you just read a monotonous script without putting your soul into it, the audience will immediately sense it, and the connection will break. Emotions are what create an indissoluble bond between you and your audience, and this bond is what makes podcasting such a powerful medium.

There's a big difference between listening to someone reciting a script and listening to someone speaking as if they're chatting with a friend. When you listen to a podcast where the host seems stiff or cold, you likely feel distant, disengaged. But when you listen to a podcast where the host laughs, makes spontaneous jokes, makes mistakes and then corrects themselves with a chuckle, you feel involved. You feel like you're part of that conversation, as if you're experiencing that moment with the host.

There's nothing wrong with being human. In fact, that's exactly what people seek. People don't want to listen to a perfect robot; they want to listen to someone who makes mistakes, laughs, and shows their emotions. It's this authenticity that keeps them hooked to episodes and makes them return for more because they feel they have a real connection with you. Vulnerability isn't a weakness but a strength. Admitting a mistake, telling a personal story, showing your emotions—these things not only make your podcast more interesting but also make you more authentic and closer to your audience.

An Example of Authenticity

Have you ever listened to a podcast where the host just seemed to be reciting a script? The voice sounds flat, monotonous, lacking warmth. Even if the content is interesting, it lacks that energy, that spark that makes you want to keep listening. Now think of another podcast where the host laughs, makes spontaneous jokes, mispronounces a word, and corrects themselves while laughing. Maybe they interrupt the flow of the conversation to share a personal anecdote. Which one made you feel more engaged? Probably the second one because that's where you heard the authentic voice of a real person, not an automated reader.

This example shows that you don't need to be perfect to be effective. You don't need to worry about seeming impeccable or avoiding every tiny mistake. People appreciate the genuineness of a smile or a spontaneous laugh more than a perfectly constructed performance.

Turning the Podcast into a Conversation

Start thinking of your podcast as a chat between friends. You don't need excessive formality, nor do you need a distant or overly professional tone. Formality risks creating a gap between you and your listeners, and that's not what you want. You want your audience to feel as though they're sitting next to you, as though they're part of the conversation. The more open, sincere, and vulnerable you show yourself to be, the more your audience will feel connected to you, and the more likely they'll continue to follow you.

In the end, being authentic means being yourself. Don't be afraid to show who you really are. Don't be afraid to make mistakes, laugh at yourself, or share a part of your life. That's what makes a podcast truly special and unique. The audience doesn't want to listen to a perfected version of you; they want to listen to you—with all your imperfections, emotions, and authenticity.

4. STAY CONSISTENT

Consistency is one of the most underrated yet crucial ingredients for building a successful podcast. At the beginning, when you're driven by the excitement and enthusiasm of creating something new, it's easy to feel invincible. Ideas seem to flow effortlessly, and passion pushes you to record episode after episode. But like any creative project, the real challenge isn't starting strong, but maintaining that momentum in the long run.

Think of podcasting as a marathon, not a sprint. It's easy to start at full speed, but if you don't manage your energy well, you risk burning out halfway through. Just like in a relationship, at the beginning everything seems new and exciting, but over time, it requires commitment, dedication, and constant work to make it function and grow. Consistency requires discipline, and it's not always easy to maintain that initial spark, especially when life or work becomes more demanding.

Consistency doesn't just apply to how often you publish new episodes but also to your overall presence for your audience. Publishing regularly allows you to create expectations and habits in your listeners. If people know they'll find a new episode every Tuesday morning, that day will become their "appointment" with you. This sense of continuity not only builds a connection with your audience but also allows you to become part of their daily routine.

Remember that consistency isn't just about the number of episodes but also about quality. It's better to release an excellent episode every two weeks than to publish two mediocre ones every week. Quality is essential to keeping your audience engaged. Regularly publishing episodes that don't meet your audience's expectations can be worse than not publishing at all. Listeners have a low tolerance for low-quality content, and they may quickly abandon you if they sense a decline in the standard of your episodes.

Time and Energy Management

One of the most common mistakes is overestimating your ability to maintain a tight publishing schedule. At first, you might be tempted to publish an episode a day or three times a week, thinking that the more content you produce, the faster you'll grow. This approach can quickly lead to burnout. The initial enthusiasm can fade, along with the quality and effort you put into your episodes. The result? You might find yourself skipping episodes or, worse, abandoning the project altogether.

The key is to find a sustainable pace. If you know you only have a few hours a week to dedicate to the podcast, plan accordingly. Maybe release an episode every two weeks, but make sure each episode is of high quality and worth the wait. Consistency doesn't just mean publishing often; it means publishing predictably and keeping your promise to the audience.

Being Present for Your Audience

Consistency, however, isn't limited to publishing. It also means being regularly present and available for your audience. Respond to comments, interact with your listeners on social media, and participate in the conversations that develop around your episodes. The more you make your audience feel involved and part of your community, the more attached they will become to you and will continue to follow you.

When you show that you're consistent in your commitment, it demonstrates to the audience that you truly care about them. You're there for them not only when you release new episodes but also between releases, building a relationship that goes beyond just content consumption. Think about how you feel when someone you admire responds to your comment or answers a question. It creates a sense of reciprocity and appreciation that strengthens the connection between you and your audience.

The Importance of Predictability

There's an important psychological aspect to consistency: predictability. People love knowing what to expect and when. This applies to all media, but it's especially true for podcasts. Imagine you're following a podcast you love, published with a certain regularity. It becomes part of your routine, something you look forward to every week. Then, suddenly, the episodes start coming out irregularly. One day there's an episode, then nothing for two weeks, and then another episode. You'd feel disoriented, and probably, you'd start looking for another podcast that can provide the continuity you're missing.

Trust is also built through regularity. If the audience knows they can count on you, that they'll consistently find new high-quality episodes, they'll keep coming back. But if they start to feel that you don't have a clear plan or that you don't take your commitment seriously, that trust will erode. And once listeners stop trusting you, it's hard to win them back.

Consistency Is Respect

Finally, consistency is a form of respect towards your listeners. Regularly publishing shows that you take your podcast seriously, as well as your audience and the commitment you've made to them. It's not just about adhering to a release schedule but about showing that you care about your listeners' experience.

People dedicate their time to your podcast: they listen during the free moments of their day, whether during short breaks at work, while running, or before falling asleep. Knowing that you're consistent in your efforts makes the audience feel valued. If you show dedication, they'll repay you with loyalty and by sharing your work.

In conclusion, consistency is one of the most important elements for building a successful podcast, and paradoxically, it's also one of the hardest to maintain. It requires continuous effort, planning, and the willingness not to give in to the impulse to do everything at once. Consistency is the bridge that builds trust and the relationship with your audience, and without it, even the best content can go unnoticed.

5. LISTEN TO FEEDBACK

The final essential element for a successful podcast is feedback. This term often evokes mixed reactions: some see it as a challenge, others as an opportunity. But one thing is certain: you can't grow if you don't listen to your audience. When you create something—whether it's a podcast, an article, or any other type of content—you are inevitably immersed in your own vision. You're so close to your project that it's easy to lose sight of certain things, no matter how passionate and dedicated you are. This is where feedback comes in: it's the window that allows you to see your creation through the eyes of those who listen to you.

Every time you receive a comment, a review, or even a simple email, you're gaining a perspective that you, as the creator, don't have. Your audience can notice details, nuances, or even issues that might escape your attention. They may perceive a tone you didn't intend to convey or realize that a topic you thought was well-covered wasn't understood as clearly as you hoped. This is the power of feedback: it allows you to improve what you do, grow, and evolve as a podcaster.

It's important to note that not all feedback will be useful or constructive. Some will be simply personal preferences, while others may be criticisms that aren't well-argued. However, it's crucial to know how to listen and filter. As in any type of communication, you need to read between the lines, distinguishing between constructive criticism and reactions based on subjective tastes.

Some listeners might suggest shorter episodes, while others may want longer ones. Both types of feedback can be valid, but it doesn't mean you have to follow every recommendation. You must always balance what you're being told with your own vision and style. You don't need to please everyone, but you do need to be open to change and growth, always considering what can strengthen your connection with the audience.

The Value of Criticism

Criticism, especially constructive criticism, is the most valuable feedback you can receive. It's never easy to accept criticism, especially when you've invested so much time and energy into a project, but it's often from those comments that the most significant improvements come. It could be criticism about the pacing of your narration, the audio quality, or how you approach a particular topic. These comments, even if they might hurt your ego, are essential for helping you improve. Learning to see them as opportunities rather than personal attacks is a crucial part of the growth process.

Remember that those who criticize you do so because they took the time to listen, and this means that, in some way, they found value in your podcast. Even criticism can be seen as a form of appreciation: if someone weren't interested, they wouldn't take the trouble to give you feedback.

Handling Negative Feedback

Managing negative feedback can be difficult, but it's a fundamental skill for a successful podcaster. Your first reaction might be defensive, especially when you feel the criticism is unjustified. But it's important to take a step back, reflect, and try to understand the listener's point of view. Sometimes, negative feedback is simply a matter of personal taste, while other times it can reveal gaps you hadn't noticed.

One effective way to handle negative feedback is to respond with openness and humility. Thanking the listener for sharing their opinion is the first step. You don't have to agree with it, but showing that you appreciate the time and effort they took to write to you can strengthen your relationship with the audience. Always be open to dialogue: your audience appreciates a podcaster who is willing to listen, even when the feedback isn't positive.

The Role of Positive Feedback

On the other hand, positive feedback is just as important, if not more. It's easy to focus on criticism and overlook compliments, but the latter are crucial for keeping your motivation high and understanding what you're doing well. When your audience tells you that they found a particular episode insightful or that your voice accompanied them during a tough time, you're receiving invaluable information. Positive feedback tells you what to continue doing and confirms that you're on the right path.

Once again, interacting with those who leave positive comments is important. Thank those who appreciate your work, show them that their opinion matters, and let them know that their support motivates you to continue. These small gestures create a community around your podcast and make your audience feel part of something special. There's nothing more rewarding for a listener than knowing their voice was heard.

Creating Spaces for Feedback

But how do you get feedback effectively? Often, the audience doesn't leave reviews spontaneously, so it's up to you to create the spaces to encourage them to do so. During your episodes, don't hesitate to ask direct questions to your audience: "What do you think about this topic? Do you have suggestions for future episodes?" These questions, even if they seem simple, can invite listeners to reflect and interact with you.

Also, make sure it's easy for your audience to give you feedback. Create a dedicated email or a form on your website. Use social platforms to gather opinions and stimulate discussions. You can even run polls to get a clear idea of your audience's preferences. The more accessible you make this process, the more feedback you'll get, and the more you'll be able to improve and grow your podcast.

The Podcast as a Community

Finally, feedback helps turn your podcast into something bigger than just a show: it can become a community. When you invite listeners to share their opinions, contribute ideas, or interact with you, you make them an active part of your project. They're no longer just passive listeners but participants. This creates a deep bond that goes beyond mere passive listening. Your podcast isn't just a one-way conversation but an ongoing dialogue between you and your audience.

A successful podcast isn't just a collection of well-recorded episodes; it's a community of people who feel connected through the stories, ideas, and conversations you present. And feedback is the tool that allows you to nurture and grow this community.

In conclusion, feedback isn't just an optional component in podcasting; it's a vital resource for improving, evolving, and building a strong bond with your audience. Knowing how to listen, respond, and adapt to the opinions and suggestions of those who follow you will make the difference between a static podcast and one that is dynamic and constantly evolving

6. CHOOSE THE RIGHT NICHE

One of the key factors for the success of a podcast is choosing the right niche. In a world saturated with content, with thousands of podcasts available on almost every imaginable topic, finding your unique space is essential to stand out from the crowd. The temptation might be to talk about everything, covering various subjects and trying to reach a broader audience. However, this strategy often backfires. You can't speak to everyone. Trying to do so risks making your message superficial and uninteresting because you fail to meet the specific needs of any audience in depth. The key to success is being specific.

Choosing a well-defined niche means narrowing the focus of your podcast to a particular topic that you're passionate about, have expertise in, and that can attract a specific, engaged audience. A well-chosen niche doesn't limit your possibilities but amplifies them. It allows you to become a reference point for a group of listeners who share your interests and who are looking for exactly that type of content.

When selecting your niche, you need to think long-term. Who are the people I want to reach? What are their interests, needs, and concerns? The more you can answer these questions, the better you'll be able to create content that resonates with your audience. People seek content that speaks to them, their desires, and their problems. If you can provide this, you will build a strong, lasting connection with those who listen to you.

The Power of Specialization

Focusing on a niche allows you to become a recognized expert in that specific field. Being too general makes you anonymous, while specializing helps you build a strong identity and clear positioning. The more you focus on a specific topic, the more recognizable you become. People know exactly what to expect from your podcast and will know that you are the right person to listen to for in-depth coverage of that particular theme.

Specialization also helps you create more targeted and detailed content. You won't find yourself having to cover too many topics superficially, but you'll be able to dive deep, offering insights and knowledge that more general podcasts can't provide. This makes you more valuable in the eyes of your audience because you offer something unique that's hard to find elsewhere.

Another advantage of specialization is that it helps you build a community around your podcast. When you focus on a niche topic, you attract people with similar interests who share a common passion. These people won't just be passive listeners but will become active members of your community, participating in discussions, sharing your episodes, and helping your show grow.

The Niche Is Not a Limitation

One of the mistakes many podcasters make is thinking that narrowing down their niche limits their growth potential. In reality, it's the exact opposite. When you focus on a specific topic, you attract a more engaged and loyal audience, who will continue to follow you over time because they recognize the unique value of your content.

Even if it might seem at first that speaking to a small slice of the audience limits your opportunities, it's precisely this specialized audience that will allow you to grow organically. People who find value in your content will be more likely to share your podcast with others, creating a ripple effect that will help you expand. Your reputation will be built not on quantity but on the quality of the connection you create with your niche audience.

Moreover, starting with a niche doesn't mean you're bound to a single topic forever. Once you've built a solid base of loyal listeners, you can gradually expand your scope, introducing new topics or broadening your podcast's focus. But the starting point must be a precise niche that allows you to create a strong, recognizable identity.

How to Choose the Right Niche

Choosing a niche isn't always easy, but there are some questions that can guide you in the right direction. What are your interests and passions? What are your areas of expertise? Are there already many podcasts that cover this topic? If so, how can you offer a unique perspective or added value?

A good starting point is to focus on what you're passionate about. If you talk about a topic you love, your enthusiasm will come through in every episode, and this will engage your audience. Also, being passionate about the subject will help you maintain consistency over time, avoiding losing interest or motivation.

You should also consider the skills you have. In what field do you possess knowledge that can genuinely enrich your audience? Perhaps you have professional experience in a specific sector, or you've had personal experiences that make you an expert in a particular subject. Whatever your background, use it to create content that offers value.

Finally, evaluate the competition. If there are already many podcasts covering the topic you've chosen, find a way to stand out. What can you offer that others don't? Can you adopt a different tone, bring in specialized guests, or focus on an even more specific subcategory? Your uniqueness is the key to emerging in a competitive market.

Example: The Power of a Niche

Imagine you're passionate about travel, but instead of creating a podcast about travel in general, you decide to focus on a specific sector: eco-friendly travel for families. This choice allows you to attract a very specific audience— families who want to travel while respecting the environment—and enables you to provide content tailored to their needs. You could discuss eco-friendly destinations, offer tips on how to travel with children without impacting the environment, or talk about sustainable travel products.

In this way, your podcast immediately stands out from thousands of other travel podcasts and creates a deeper connection with a specific audience. People who share these values will be much more likely to follow you faithfully, comment on your episodes, interact with you on social media, and share your podcast with other parents interested in eco-friendly travel.

The Niche as a Launchpad

The niche is the launchpad for building your identity as a podcaster and for making yourself known to the right audience. Don't be afraid to narrow your initial focus: it's a winning strategy to differentiate yourself and attract engaged, loyal listeners. Over time, you can expand your content and grow organically, but everything starts with your ability to choose the right niche and specialize.

A successful podcast doesn't aim to please everyone but offers unique and deep value to a well-defined audience. When you find your niche, you find your place in the podcasting world.

7. EXPERIMENT WITH FORMATS AND LENGTH

A successful podcast is not static. Evolving and experimenting are fundamental parts of the creative process, and one of the most effective ways to keep your audience's interest alive is to play with the formats and length of your episodes. Finding the right balance between stability and innovation allows you to offer variety to your listeners without losing coherence with your show's theme and style.

Many podcasters start with a clear idea of the format and duration they intend to follow, but over time they realize that making changes can open up new opportunities. Rigidity in structure can lead to monotony, both for you and your listeners, whereas introducing variations, testing new approaches, or adjusting episode length can be stimulating and surprising for the audience.

Why Experimentation is Important

Experimenting with formats and length allows you to keep your audience engaged and curious. If you always release episodes with the same structure and length, you risk becoming predictable and, consequently, losing some of the initial excitement your audience felt. Changing the format or duration from time to time not only keeps things interesting but also allows you to better adapt to your listeners' needs, who may prefer shorter episodes in certain situations or more in-depth discussions at other times.

The world of podcasting is incredibly diverse, and every audience has its preferences: some enjoy quick, informative bites, while others appreciate long, detailed conversations. Offering different options to your listeners allows you to broaden your reach and satisfy a wider range of preferences, all while keeping your loyal audience happy.

Types of Formats

Experimenting with formats means playing with the structure of your podcast. For example, if you've been using a purely narrative style, you could try introducing interviews with guests who bring new perspectives and enrich your content. Alternatively, you might experiment with thematic episodes, where you explore a topic in-depth with different guests or segments, or create a series of episodes in installments, building a more complex narrative over several episodes.

Another idea is to alternate between episodes where you share your reflections and expertise alone and episodes with a co-host or guests. The dynamics of interaction can offer a different rhythm and attract an audience that prefers a more dialogue-based format.

Q&A episodes (questions and answers) are another format that encourages interaction with your audience. You can ask your listeners to send in questions on a specific topic and dedicate an entire episode to providing in-depth answers, fostering a stronger connection with your community.

Consider also adding special episodes, such as those dedicated to specific events, thematic deep dives inspired by recent news, or reflections on current trends. The key is to maintain your unique voice and recognizable style but without being afraid to change the format from time to time.

Does an Ideal Length Exist?

One of the questions many podcasters ask themselves is what the ideal episode length is. In reality, there is no one-size-fits-all answer because the perfect length depends on several factors: the theme of the podcast, the target audience, the episode's content, and the format you use. Some listeners prefer short episodes that easily fit into their busy days, perhaps during their commute or lunch break. Others enjoy devoting more time to long, detailed episodes, ideal for more relaxed listening sessions or during activities like walking, exercising, or driving.

The key is to find a balance and experiment to see what length works best for your audience. If your podcast has always featured 30-minute episodes, try introducing a 15-minute episode and see how your audience reacts. You can also alternate between short and long episodes: a short episode to provide a quick overview of a topic and a longer one for a more in-depth analysis.

A good way to guide yourself is to listen to your audience's feedback. You might discover that some prefer concise, straightforward episodes, while others appreciate long, leisurely conversations. The important thing is not to force the length: if a topic requires more time to explore, don't be afraid to give it the time it deserves. Conversely, if an episode can be resolved in less time, don't stretch it out just to meet a certain length. Quality is always more important than quantity.

Example: How to Vary Episode Length

Imagine that your podcast usually runs about 45 minutes per episode. One day, you decide to experiment: you create a special 10-minute episode, focusing on a quick update or a personal reflection. This shorter episode can be easily consumed by those with limited time but could also spark curiosity about longer episodes, encouraging listeners to explore more of your podcast. Variety in episode length allows you to offer flexibility to listeners, who can choose to listen to you at the times that best fit their routines.

At the same time, you could create longer episodes in the form of in-depth interviews, exploring a topic in great detail. The important thing is not to be afraid to step outside your comfort zone: there's no rigid rule on episode length, but there is one rule on quality. If what you have to say is worth 10 minutes, say it in 10 minutes. If you need an hour, take that hour.

Finding Your Balance

Experimenting with formats and episode length doesn't mean completely overhauling your podcast but rather adapting and optimizing your offering to keep your audience's attention alive while also keeping your motivation high. Try new things, monitor reactions, and adjust as you receive feedback.

Remember: innovation is part of the creative process. Don't be afraid to change the structure, length, or format of your episodes. Every podcast is unique and has its own natural evolution. Podcasting is a versatile and dynamic medium, and your ability to experiment will keep your audience engaged and curious about what you have in store.

In conclusion, the format and length of your podcast shouldn't be seen as fixed rules but as tools of expression that you can adjust according to the content, theme, and preferences of your audience. Experiment, play with options, and let your podcast evolve with you.

8. LEARN TO PROMOTE YOUR PODCAST

Creating quality content is essential, but just as important is making sure people know about your podcast. Promotion plays a crucial role in bringing your show to the attention of the audience. You could have the best podcast in the world, but if no one knows about it, it will be hard to build a listener base. Effectively promoting your podcast is a process that requires strategy, planning, and consistency, but it's also an opportunity to grow your community and reach new listeners.

Why Promotion is Important

Today, there are thousands of podcasts available on every imaginable topic. This means that no matter how interesting or well-produced your show is, it won't be discovered by chance. Promotion is not just about getting more listeners but also about creating visibility and recognition in your sector. A good marketing strategy allows you to expand your audience, grow your reputation, and establish a stronger connection with both your current and potential listeners.

Promoting a podcast isn't a one-time action that you can set and forget. It requires a continuous and diversified approach, using various channels and platforms to reach potential listeners. Whether it's social media, collaborations with other podcasters, or using specialized platforms, promoting your podcast strategically is essential for its long-term success.

Effective Promotion Strategies

1. Use Social Media: Social media is one of the most powerful tools to get your podcast noticed. You can create dedicated content to promote each new episode, such as engaging audio clips, graphics, or interesting quotes from the episodes. Platforms like Instagram, Twitter, TikTok, and LinkedIn allow you to reach a wide audience, but it's important to tailor your message to each platform's tone. On social media, don't just announce a new episode's release —engage with the community, ask questions, spark conversations, and use relevant hashtags to reach new listeners.

2. Collaborate with Other Podcasters: Another effective tactic is collaborating with other podcasters in your sector or in related niches. Guest swapping, where you appear on someone else's podcast and they appear on yours, allows you to tap into an already loyal audience that might be interested in your content. This type of collaboration not only increases your visibility but also helps you build valuable relationships within the podcasting community. Additionally, you can organize crossover episodes, where two podcasts tackle the same topic from different perspectives, offering added value to both audiences.

3. Create a Dedicated Website: Having a website dedicated to your podcast is another essential promotional tool. The website not only serves as an archive for all your episodes but also offers a place where your audience can learn more about you, your guests, and the topics you cover. You can also create a blog associated with your podcast, where you delve deeper into the topics discussed in episodes or offer additional resources like links, articles, and recommended books. The website is a space you control entirely and can use to improve your podcast's SEO, making it easier for people to discover through searches.

4. Newsletter and Mailing List: Newsletters are an incredibly powerful tool for promoting new episodes and keeping your audience up to date. If you haven't already, create a mailing list and send periodic newsletters to your subscribers. In addition to promoting new episodes, you can use the newsletter to share personal insights, offer deeper reflections, or answer audience questions. This helps build a stronger bond with listeners, who will feel they have a direct line of communication with you. Newsletters are effective because they reach people directly in their inbox, creating a more intimate and personal connection compared to social media.

5. Optimize Your Podcast's SEO: SEO (Search Engine Optimization) isn't just for websites; it applies to podcasts too. Every time you publish a new episode, make sure to optimize the titles, descriptions, and keywords used to make your podcast easily visible in search engines and on podcast platforms. Use relevant keywords that reflect the episode's theme, and write detailed descriptions that clearly explain what it's about. This will help people who are searching for specific content find your show and decide to listen.

6. Participate in Events and Conferences: Attending industry events and conferences (both online and offline) allows you to meet other professionals and potential listeners who are interested in your topics. You can present your podcast, offer talks or workshops, or simply network to get your show noticed. Many conferences now include sections dedicated to podcasters, where you can promote your episodes or talk about your experience.

Engage with the Podcasting Community

The podcasting community is constantly growing. Being part of this network of podcasters and listeners is a great strategy to promote your show. Participate in discussion groups, forums, and communities dedicated to podcasting. In these spaces, you can share your episodes, exchange advice and ideas with other podcasters, join discussions on topics of interest, and increase your visibility.

Example of Strategic Promotion

Imagine you've just launched a new episode on a particularly timely and interesting topic for your niche. The promotion could follow this approach:

1. Create a teaser clip of the episode and post it on social media, accompanied by eye-catching graphics and a short text that piques curiosity.
2. Promote the episode in your newsletter, providing personal insights on the topic discussed.
3. Collaborate with another podcaster on a crossover episode, where both of you talk about the same topic from different angles and share your content on each other's platforms.
4. Optimize the episode's title and description with SEO keywords, making it more easily visible on podcasting platforms.
5. Share the episode in relevant online discussion groups, engaging the audience in the conversation.

This integrated approach allows you to reach your audience through multiple channels and formats, maximizing the episode's visibility and building an increasingly engaged listener base.

Promoting your podcast is essential for growing your audience and showcasing the value of your work. It's not enough to create quality content; you must ensure people can find and be attracted to it. A good promotional strategy allows you to expand your reach, build stronger connections with your audience, and turn occasional listeners into loyal fans.

9. MONETIZE SUSTAINABLY

One of the primary goals for many podcasters, especially once they've built a solid listener base, is to monetize their show. Turning your podcast into a source of income is an important step, but it requires strategy and a deep understanding of the various monetization methods available. It's essential to find a balance between earning money and maintaining your audience's trust and respect, avoiding overwhelming them with sponsored or overly commercial content.

Monetizing a podcast sustainably means finding an approach that not only allows you to generate revenue but also aligns with your values and the expectations of your audience. Not all forms of monetization are suitable for every podcast; some might work for you, while others might not. The important thing is to be aware of the options available and to choose those that best fit your show, without compromising the quality of the content.

Why It's Important to Monetize Sustainably

Sustainability in monetization is essential to avoid alienating your audience. Listeners connect to your podcast because they're interested in the content you offer, and an overly commercial approach could damage that connection. At the same time, monetization must be justified by the value you provide: if your podcast is a valuable resource for your listeners, it's fair to seek financial return for the time and effort you invest in creating content.

A sustainable approach to monetization means being transparent with your audience about how and why you're seeking to monetize. If listeners feel that you're monetizing purely for personal gain, without providing value in return, they may distance themselves. On the other hand, if you show that the revenue allows you to improve the podcast or continue producing high-quality content, the audience will be more inclined to support you.

Sustainable Monetization Methods

1. Sponsorships and Advertising: One of the most common forms of monetization is incorporating sponsorships or advertisements into your podcast. However, it's important to do this thoughtfully. When looking for sponsors, seek out brands or companies that align with your podcast's values and that are relevant to your audience. Avoid including ads that may seem out of place or forced. For example, if your podcast is about health and wellness, you might partner with brands that offer natural supplements or fitness equipment rather than companies unrelated to the topic. This way, the sponsorships become a natural extension of your content and don't disrupt the listening experience.

When integrating ads, try to be creative in how you present them. You could, for example, include native ads, where the advertisement blends seamlessly with the episode's content. This allows you to maintain the natural flow of conversation and makes the advertising message less intrusive. Always be transparent with your audience: disclosing that a segment is sponsored builds trust and demonstrates professionalism.

2. Crowdfunding and Donations: If you prefer to keep your podcast free from ads, you might consider crowdfunding or direct donations. Platforms like Patreon, Ko-fi, or Buy Me a Coffee allow you to ask for direct support from your audience, offering them the opportunity to contribute financially to the podcast's production in exchange for exclusive content, early access, or other perks.

Crowdfunding is an effective way to monetize sustainably, especially if you have a loyal community that appreciates the value of your work. It allows your audience to feel involved in the podcast's success and growth, fostering a deeper connection between you and your listeners.

3. Merchandise: Another way to monetize your podcast is through selling merchandise. Branded items such as t-shirts, mugs, or stickers can be a fun and effective way to generate revenue while promoting your podcast. Merchandise gives your listeners a tangible way to support you and can serve as a marketing tool, spreading awareness of your show to new potential listeners.

4. Premium Content: Offering exclusive content to paying subscribers is another sustainable monetization option. You can create a separate tier of content, such as bonus episodes, behind-the-scenes insights, or early access to episodes, available only to subscribers. This can be done through platforms like Patreon or subscription services on major podcasting platforms. Offering premium content allows you to provide additional value to your most dedicated listeners while still maintaining free content for your wider audience.

5. Affiliate Marketing: Affiliate marketing allows you to earn a commission by promoting products or services that you genuinely believe in. By recommending products relevant to your audience and including affiliate links, you can generate income when listeners purchase through your referral. The key to affiliate marketing is authenticity: only promote products you've personally used or that you believe align with your podcast's theme and audience interests. This ensures that your recommendations are trustworthy and beneficial to your listeners.

6. Live Events and Webinars: As your podcast grows, you might consider organizing live events, workshops, or webinars for your audience. These events can be monetized through ticket sales, sponsorships, or donations. Live events offer a way to engage more deeply with your audience, create a sense of community, and provide unique value that goes beyond the typical podcast format.

Transparency and Trust

Regardless of the monetization method you choose, transparency with your audience is key. Always clearly communicate why and how you are monetizing your podcast. Whether it's to cover production costs, improve the show's quality, or compensate for the time and effort you put into the project, your listeners will appreciate your honesty.

Trust is the foundation of a successful podcast, and it's essential that your audience feels that their support contributes to maintaining or enhancing the quality of the content they enjoy. The moment listeners feel that monetization is compromising the authenticity or value of your show, the relationship you've built could be at risk.

Example of Sustainable Monetization

Imagine you've been running a podcast about personal development for a few years, and now you've built a loyal following. You decide to introduce sustainable monetization through a mix of strategies:

1. You start a Patreon page where listeners can support you financially in exchange for exclusive bonus content and early access to episodes.
2. You partner with a few carefully selected sponsors, such as brands that

offer meditation apps or self-help books, integrating their ads naturally into the podcast.

3. You launch a small merchandise line with branded items that resonate with your podcast's theme.

4. You occasionally organize live webinars, offering in-depth discussions on personal development topics, with tickets available for purchase.

This approach allows you to diversify your revenue streams without overwhelming your audience with excessive commercial content, ensuring that monetization supports the podcast's growth while maintaining its integrity.

In Conclusion

Monetizing your podcast sustainably is an achievable goal, but it requires a thoughtful strategy and a clear understanding of your audience. The key is to find methods that align with your values and those of your listeners, ensuring that monetization enhances, rather than detracts from, the overall podcast experience. By being transparent and maintaining trust, you can create a podcast that not only succeeds financially but continues to deliver value to your audience.

10. STAY UPDATED

Podcasting is a rapidly evolving field, and to remain relevant, you need to stay updated on the latest trends, tools, and best practices. The world of podcasting doesn't stand still: new technologies, platforms, and audience preferences are constantly emerging, and keeping up with these changes is essential for continuing to offer high-quality content.

Staying updated means more than just being aware of the latest podcasting software or editing techniques. It involves keeping a finger on the pulse of industry trends, audience behavior, and content formats that are gaining popularity. Being adaptable and open to learning allows you to evolve as a podcaster and meet the ever-changing expectations of your audience.

The Importance of Continuous Learning

Podcasting is a craft that requires ongoing development. Even the most experienced podcasters continue to learn and refine their skills over time. Whether it's discovering a new way to structure your episodes, adopting innovative editing techniques, or experimenting with different promotional strategies, being open to learning will keep your podcast fresh and engaging.

One of the best ways to stay updated is by listening to other podcasts, both within your niche and beyond. Pay attention to how successful podcasters structure their episodes, how they engage with their audience, and how they integrate new trends into their shows. By observing what works well for others, you can gain valuable insights and ideas to apply to your own podcast.

Embrace New Technologies and Tools

Technology plays a huge role in podcasting, and new tools are constantly being developed to improve sound quality, streamline editing, or enhance promotion. Staying updated with the latest technology can give you a significant edge, allowing you to produce more professional and polished content.

For example, investing in better recording equipment, using advanced editing software, or adopting AI-powered tools for sound editing and transcription can significantly improve the overall quality of your podcast. Additionally, many new platforms and services can help you promote your podcast more effectively or monetize it more easily. Keeping an eye on these innovations and integrating them into your process can save you time and effort while improving the listener experience.

Understanding Your Audience's Changing Preferences

Audience preferences are not static. What listeners find engaging today might not hold the same appeal tomorrow. Therefore, staying updated also means paying close attention to your audience's behavior and interests. Use analytics tools to track listener engagement, such as which episodes perform best, the average listening time, and the demographics of your audience. This data will help you adapt your content to meet the preferences and needs of your listeners.

In addition to analytics, regularly interacting with your audience through social media, emails, or live events can provide valuable insights into what they want more of or what isn't working. Understanding these changes allows you to stay relevant and continue to grow your listener base.

Following Industry Trends

The podcasting industry is constantly evolving, with new formats, platforms, and monetization models emerging all the time. For example, short-form podcasts have become increasingly popular, offering quick, bite-sized content that fits into people's busy lives. On the other hand, there's also a growing trend toward long-form, deep-dive podcasts that explore complex topics in great detail. Knowing these trends allows you to experiment with new formats that could attract a wider audience or better meet the needs of your current listeners.

It's also important to stay informed about platform-specific trends. Podcast platforms like Spotify, Apple Podcasts, and YouTube are constantly updating their features and algorithms. Understanding how these platforms prioritize content, promote shows, and reach new audiences is critical for optimizing your podcast for discoverability.

Engaging with the Podcasting Community

One of the best ways to stay updated is to engage with the broader podcasting community. Join podcasting forums, attend industry events, and participate in online discussions with other podcasters. These communities are excellent resources for exchanging ideas, learning about new trends, and discovering the latest tools and technologies.

Conferences and workshops, whether in-person or online, offer opportunities to hear from experts, learn about industry advancements, and network with other podcasters. Staying connected with the community not only keeps you informed but also opens up collaboration opportunities that can help you grow your podcast.

The Importance of Adaptability

Remaining adaptable is key to thriving in the dynamic world of podcasting. The ability to pivot, try new things, and evolve with changing trends will set your podcast apart and ensure it continues to grow. This doesn't mean you should chase every new trend or abandon your core style, but rather that you should remain open to exploring new possibilities and adjusting your approach when it benefits your audience.

Staying updated doesn't mean sacrificing your identity as a podcaster, but it does mean being aware of the shifts in the landscape and adapting your content and strategy accordingly. The best podcasters strike a balance between staying true to their voice and being open to new methods, technologies, and ideas that can enhance their work.

Example: Adapting to Changes in the Podcasting Landscape

Imagine you've been running a podcast for a few years with a loyal audience. Over time, you notice that listeners are increasingly interested in shorter, more concise episodes. While your podcast traditionally runs an hour per episode, you decide to experiment by creating 15-minute versions of the same content, providing a quick summary or key takeaways for those with less time. At the same time, you invest in new sound editing tools that allow you to streamline the editing process, improving sound quality while saving time. By staying updated and adapting to the changing landscape, you maintain your audience's engagement and attract new listeners who prefer a shorter format.

In Conclusion

Staying updated is an essential part of being a successful podcaster. By embracing new technologies, understanding audience preferences, following industry trends, and engaging with the podcasting community, you ensure that your podcast remains relevant and continues to grow. Podcasting is a dynamic medium, and the more you learn and evolve, the more you'll be able to provide valuable content that resonates with your audience.

CONCLUSION: PODCASTING AS A JOURNEY

Podcasting is much more than a platform for disseminating information; it's an art form, a means of communication that allows you to connect with an audience in a profound and meaningful way. Throughout this book, we've explored the key elements that contribute to a successful podcast: creating valuable content, maintaining audio quality, being authentic, staying consistent, listening to feedback, choosing the right niche, experimenting with formats and length, promoting your show, monetizing sustainably, and staying updated.

However, beyond all these practical aspects, podcasting is, at its core, a journey. It's a path of constant growth and discovery, both for you as a creator and for your listeners. Every episode, every conversation, and every interaction with your audience is a new opportunity to evolve and deepen the connection you've built with those who follow you.

What makes podcasting special is the intimacy it creates between the podcaster and the audience. Your voice becomes a companion for your listeners, accompanying them through their daily lives, offering insights, entertainment, and, often, comfort. This relationship is what sets podcasting apart from other forms of media: it's not just about broadcasting a message, but about building a relationship, episode by episode, with those who choose to listen to you.

The Value of Perseverance

Like any creative endeavor, podcasting requires perseverance. There will be challenges along the way—moments when inspiration runs low, technical issues arise, or growth seems stagnant. But it's precisely in these moments that your passion and commitment will make the difference. Continuing to produce content, engage with your audience, and refine your approach will pay off in the long run.

It's also important to remember that success in podcasting doesn't happen overnight. Building a loyal audience takes time, as does mastering the technical and creative aspects of the medium. But with patience, dedication, and a willingness to learn and adapt, the rewards will come, both in terms of personal satisfaction and in the growth of your podcast.

The Future of Podcasting

Podcasting is a constantly evolving medium, and its future holds endless possibilities. New platforms, technologies, and formats are emerging all the time, offering podcasters more tools and opportunities to reach a wider audience. As a podcaster, staying curious and open to new developments will allow you to take full advantage of these opportunities and continue to offer content that resonates with your listeners.

But beyond the technical and logistical aspects, the future of podcasting will continue to be driven by the most important element: the relationship between podcasters and their audiences. As long as you remain true to your voice, listen to your listeners, and continue to offer value in each episode, your podcast will remain relevant and appreciated.

Final Thoughts

Podcasting is a rewarding and enriching experience that allows you to share your ideas, stories, and passions with the world. Whether you're just starting out or have been podcasting for years, the key to success lies in staying authentic, listening to your audience, and continuously evolving.

As you move forward in your podcasting journey, keep in mind that there's no single path to success. Every podcast is unique, just as every podcaster is. Find your voice, connect with your audience, and enjoy the journey—because ultimately, podcasting is about much more than just producing content. It's about creating something meaningful that resonates with others and builds a lasting connection.

Thank you for reading, and I wish you the best of luck in your podcasting endeavors!

About the Author

Alessandro Mazzù is a podcasting expert and content creator with over a decade of experience in the field. He has helped numerous brands and individuals launch and grow their podcasts, offering valuable insights on content creation, promotion, and audience engagement. With a passion for storytelling and communication, Alessandro's work has been featured on various platforms, and he continues to contribute to the podcasting community through workshops, webinars, and consulting services.